This book belongs to...

Name:..

Age:..

Published by Dennis Publishing Ltd. 30 Cleveland St, London W1T 4JD. Company registered in England. www.dennis.co.uk

DISCLAIMER
The screenshots shown in this publication were taken from Minecraft, a game published by Mojang Synergies AB. Game design, programming and graphics for Minecraft were authored by Notch, employees and/or freelancers of Mojang Synergies AB. "Minecraft" is a registered trademark of Mojang Synergies AB. This publication and its contents are not licensed, authorised or connected with Mojang Synergies or any other individuals who are authors of Minecraft. This is a 100% unofficial and independent publication.

Dennis Publishing excludes all liability for the content and service provided by and websites we review. We are not responsible for and do not endorse any advertising, products or resources available from such external resources or websites and shall not be liable to any party as a result of any information, services or resources made available through such websites.

All copyrights recognised and used specifically for the purpose of criticism and review.

MINECRAFT SECRETS & CHEATS ANNUAL 2018

WHAT'S INSIDE?!

101 BRILLIANT MINECRAFT TRICKS!
Give yourself a head start at Minecraft!
Pages 10, 34, 68

THE ADVENTURES OF CRAFTY CALLUM!
See what trouble he gets into! Pages 18 and 72

THE CRAZIEST BUILDS!
Reckon you can beat any of these?!
Page 22

THE BIG MINECRAFT QUIZ
How well do YOU know the world's best videogame?!
Page 84

AMAZING TIPS!
Get the best potions on page 38, epic recipes on page 40 and brilliant enchantments on page 42!

PUZZLES
You'll find loads of puzzles dotted around this annual – and all the answers start on page 90!

THE 10 MUST-KNOW CHARACTERS OF MINECRAFT

STEVE

First introduced to Minecraft in the very first PC version way back in December 2010, Steve was the only default skin for the player for almost four years. Steve has blue eyes and short brown hair, and wears a light blue T-shirt, blue jeans and grey shoes. The original version of Steve had a dark brown goatee beard, and this version of the skin has the nickname "Char" after the original template's filename.

ALEX

Alex was added to Minecraft in PC version 1.8 pre1, which was released in August 2014, and then quickly added to the Console and Pocket editions. Alex has green eyes and long ginger hair, which she wears in a ponytail. She wears a green tunic with a belt around the waist, brown leggings and grey boots. Her character model has thinner arms than Steve, but this is the only difference between the two.

CREEPER

The creeper is Minecraft's signature villain! These weird monsters hide in the dark, and when they see an enemy – meaning you – they hiss loudly before exploding! They don't have any mercy and can't be reasoned with, and they're scared of only one thing: cats. All you can do is avoid them or run. Minecraft's creators say that if you touched a creeper it would feel like wet leaves, but why would you get that close?!

Steve

Alex

Creeper

Witch

Zombie villager

Iron golem

WITCH

The witch was an ordinary villager until she got struck by lightning! Turned evil by the strike, she was banished from the village to live in a swamp. She had to build her hut on stilts to keep the water out, and she spends her time brewing potions in her cauldron so that she can get revenge on the villagers who cast her out!

ZOMBIE VILLAGER

When a zombie plague attacked their village, these unfortunate souls were caught and bitten. It didn't take them long to join the zombie ranks, but hope isn't lost – somewhere inside each of these zombie villagers lies the person they once were. With a little magic, some kind players are able to cure the zombie disease and bring them back to the realm of the living.

IRON GOLEM

Built by friendly villagers, the iron golem was brought to life using magic, and now protects large villages against attacks from zombies and witches, or anything else that would injure its masters.

ZOMBIE PIGMAN

The zombie pigman lives in the Nether. Half-zombie, half-pig, all it remembers is enjoying its life in the Overworld, eating potatoes and carrots, before a bright flash of light changed everything for it. Now the pigman lives in the Nether, trying to find a portal to return to the Overworld and attacking anything that gets in his way with his golden sword.

Zombie pigman

Enderman

The wither

Ender dragon

ENDERMAN

The endermen lived peacefully with one another in the End, their realm protected by the ender dragon, but one day invaders visited their world and began to take their precious artifacts, such as the elytra. Now they're fighting back, using their teleportation powers to visit the Overworld and even travelling as far as the Nether to eliminate anyone who might try to attack them.

THE WITHER

Formed from the heads of three wither skeletons and the strange soul sand that exists only in the Nether, the wither is a vengeful and dangerous creature with the ability to summon a destructive wither storm that decimates everything in its path. The keeper of the rare and powerful Nether star, it's almost impossible to defeat – just being near it makes you feel weak!

The knowledge of how to summon the wither was considered so dangerous that centuries ago the ancient inhabitants of the Overworld tried to hide it completely, but one painting gives clues as to how you might bring the wither to life. Only the very brave or incredibly stupid would try...

ENDER DRAGON

The guardian of the End, no-one knows whether the ender dragon is enslaved by the endermen, or if it was placed there to keep them from escaping their realm. Either way, its powerful attacks can only be defeated by the strongest of warriors, and its dragon's breath can power up any potion in ways few sorcerers get to try. Although the dragon can be killed, it always leaves behind an egg that can be hatched by those who know how to use the mysterious End crystals.

Be warned, though: don't ever fight the dragon if you don't expect to win, because once you're in the End there's no way out without someone dying, whether that's you or the dragon itself!

101 MINECRAFT TRICKS PART 1

D o you think you know every trick, shortcut and secret technique in Minecraft? We bet you don't, so we're going to share our expert wisdom with you. Here are 101 tricks the experts have been keeping all to themselves!

1 If you want to grow mushrooms, you can plant them on podzol and mycelium, and they'll stay where they are even in direct sunlight. Mycelium spreads to nearby dirt blocks, but podzol doesn't.

2 You might think cobblestone is useless, but it's actually one of the most useful blocks in the game and features in at least 17 recipes! So don't throw it away too quickly.

3 You can create your own grass paths by right-clicking with the shovel on grass-covered blocks (or pressing the assigned "use" button) instead of digging with it.

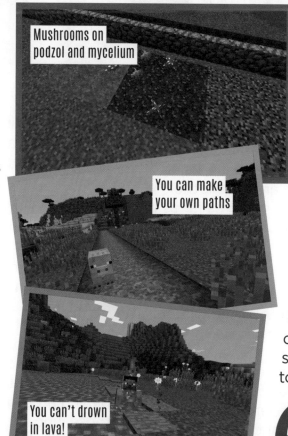

Mushrooms on podzol and mycelium

You can make your own paths

You can't drown in lava!

4 If you're not standing on something while underwater (i.e. sinking or swimming), blocks take 25 times as long to break, so don't waste your time trying to mine or dig while swimming!

5 Even though it's a liquid, it's not possible to drown in lava, though obviously you need some heavy protection to stay alive in it...!

6 Packed ice blocks don't melt even if placed next to a light source. Unfortunately, the only way to get them (except in Creative mode) is to mine them using a Silk Touch pickaxe from an ice spike, so they're very rare!

7 If you collect a raw ore block (for example, if you use a Silk Touch pickaxe) you don't have to place it then mine it again – you can smelt it into its resource.

Burn wood effectively

Jungle trees drop fewer saplings than most

Snow layers are uneven

8 Wood blocks can be used as fuel in furnaces, but it's more efficient to craft them into planks then burn them.

9 Wood planks are the single most useful block in the game, featuring in 28 different recipes.

10 Destroying a leaf block drops a sapling one in every 20 times. Jungle leaves only drop a sapling one in every 40 times.

11 Redstone ore will give off low-level light (level 9) for around a minute if struck or walked over by the player or a mob. If there's redstone nearby in a dark area, you can hit it while mining to save using up a valuable torch.

12 Snow layers can be stacked up to create partial blocks. Eight layers create a full-size snow block.

You can dry out wet sponges

Stairs save you energy

13 Even though cacti damage players and mobs that come into contact with them, you can mine cacti with your hand without taking any injuries.

14 Grass only spreads to dirt if there's a light level of at least 4 on both blocks, but mycelium only spreads to dirt if the light level is at least 9 on both blocks.

15 You can cook a wet sponge in a furnace, which will dry it out again!

16 If there's an empty bucket in the fuel slot when a furnace finishes drying out a sponge, it will turn it into a bucket of water.

17 Stairs aren't just useful for decoration or because they're compact – they also reduce your hunger stat less than jumping the same distance up or down would.

Alternate trapped and normal chests

18 Two chests placed next to each other will form a double chest, and then you have to leave a gap between a double chest and a normal chest. However, you can place a trapped chest next to a normal chest, which is a good way to maximise storage space.

19 Four iron bars in a square will create a gap big enough for the player and other mobs to drop through, but it will repel water and lava because the gap is offset from the normal block grid.

20 You can craft glowstone blocks without ever leaving the Overworld by killing witches and collecting the glowstone dust that they drop.

21 You can put carpet or snow on top of soul sand to negate its effects.

22 You can't craft cracked stone bricks, but you can turn stone bricks into cracked stone bricks by smelting them in a furnace.

23 If you fall onto a slime block, you'll bounce and won't take any damage.

24 Jack o' lanterns can be used to create snow and iron golems the same way pumpkins can.

25 Carpets let light through, so you can place carpet on top of glowstone to make a room appear illuminated even if there's no obvious light source.

26 Resource blocks like iron, gold, emerald, coal and diamond contain nine pieces of their respective resource (i.e. there are nine gold ingots in a block of gold). However, they stack in piles of 64, so you can effectively carry 576 ingots/gems in one inventory slot.

Witches drop glowstone

Slime blocks make you bounce!

Carpets let light through

Mushrooms also grow in flower pots

How to light underwater

27 Rather than putting coal in your furnaces, craft a block of coal and use that instead. It burns for as long as 10 pieces of coal would, so since it only takes nine pieces to make you technically get a bonus piece!

28 If there's a hole within six blocks of a water source block, the flow is directed towards it.

29 When you're decorating your base, remember that you can put more than just flowers in flower pots. They can also hold mushrooms, grass and ferns, saplings (which never grow) and even cacti!

30 Consider building your base in the side of a mountain. There'll be fewer ways for mobs to sneak up on you, and you'll get easy access to minerals like coal and iron ore without having to travel deep underground.

31 If you want a fire that never goes out, set Netherrack on fire. You can use this technique to create an incinerator, build a working

fireplace or just use it as some dramatic decoration.

32 If you want to light underwater, use glowstone blocks or (if you haven't reached the Nether yet) Jack o' lanterns. Both of these blocks emit light even stronger than a torch and don't get extinguished underwater.

33 You can make copies of books and maps (either for backups or sharing with other players) by crafting them with a blank version of what they are.

34 You can place a clock inside an item frame to create a wall clock, which lets you see how long you've got until it gets dark (or light!) without taking up valuable space in your inventory.

MORE ON P34

Netherrack burns forever

You can put clocks in frames

COLOUR

MEIN

Grab your pens and pencils: these two pictures need your help! Can you colour them in and make them awesome?

PUZZLE

Dot-To-Dot

Join the dots
to complete
the picture...

16

PAGES PART 1

Spot The Difference

Can you spot six changes? Good luck!

Craftygrams

Rearrange the letters to name the mobs:

1. real pa bro 2. art bib 3. leg mows on 4. shrivel ifs 5. a cam bug me
6. need merit 7. check nick joey 8. neither elk tows 9. grand red one
10. dear rail nudge

21

11 CRAZIEST MINECRAFT

11 THE EYE

This beautifully designed map offers the perfect test of your jumping skills and sense of direction. You have to navigate your way to freedom through a surreal network of platforms winding up through the sky, all under the gaze of a giant eye wearing a top hat! It's certainly weird, but thoroughly absorbing. There are plenty of parkour maps to choose from in Minecraft, but the sheer imagination in The Eye makes it one of our absolute favourites.

tinyurl.com/MCAnnual2018Build11

10 CYBORG PENGUIN

Proof that your only real limit in Minecraft is your own imagination (and spare time), here's a giant emperor penguin. But it's not just any giant emperor penguin – it has dragon wings, bandages (because it's also an Egyptian mummy), and half a metal face (because it's also a cyborg). Oh, and Minecraft user rosedragon has given it a jetpack too. Nice touch!

tinyurl.com/MCAnnual2018Build10

9 UNDERWATER CITY

Where most cities in Minecraft consist of tall, chunky blocks, Lumina Nocturnale is an inviting collection of sweeping curves and circles. All cool greys, minimal interiors and acres of glass,

BUILDS

EASTER EGG & BUNNY

8 TNT EASTER EGG AND BUNNY

Having a bad day? Then maybe watching a colossal statue of an Easter bunny explode will put a smile on your face – it certainly worked for us! The bunny and its accompanying egg are made almost entirely from TNT blocks, and detonating the thing is satisfyingly messy. Just make sure you're standing at a safe distance in Survival mode.

tinyurl.com/MCAnnual2018Build8

7 THE TEMPLE OF NOTCH

Here's a very strange build that pays homage to Markus "Notch" Persson, the creator of Minecraft. Having placed an offering in the Well of Destiny, a pair of doors open and you're confronted with a gigantic replica of Notch's bearded face. Depending on your luck, the statue's eyes will open and you'll either be showered with diamonds and gold or, more disturbingly, the floor will fall away and you'll drop into a pit of lava...

tinyurl.com/MCAnnual2018Build7

this is truly a city from the future, and what's more, it's absolutely huge! That most of the build is located underwater just makes it all the more impressive.

tinyurl.com/MCAnnual2018Build9

5 WOLF WITH TOP HAT

These days, the only people who wear top hats are posh people and magicians. But if this build is to be believed, top hats are also fashionable among wolves. To be fair, the headgear really suits this chap's face, though he does wear an expression that says, "You'd better not be laughing at my hat!"

tinyurl.com/MCAnnual2018Build5

6 ANIMAL CANNON

We're not sure how useful this is, but it looks like a lot of fun to play around with. YouTube user Kiershar has created his own animal cannon, which is capable of flinging a pig so far that it can never be found. The ingenious design uses a tower packed full of TNT to launch an animal in a minecart clear across the game map. "Pig and the minecarts were never seen again," Kiershar wrote after a test launch. "I have walked for a few Minecraft days in the direction of the launch, with no success. It's time to call off the search. RIP Pig."

tinyurl.com/MCAnnual2018Build6

4 GRABBER MACHINE

This build is a simulation of one of those grabber machines where you try (and generally fail) to pick up a stuffed toy with a wobbly metal claw. But because this is Minecraft, you control the grabber by stepping on a set of pressure plates, and the items inside the machine include creepers, witches and ocelots. Okay, so they aren't great prizes, but at least Seth's machine doesn't eat up all your spare change!

tinyurl.com/MCAnnual2018Build4

3 AUTOMATED CHICKEN FARM

Creating a plentiful, reliable source of food is one of the keys to survival in Minecraft. But what if you freed up time you'd otherwise spend harvesting food by creating your own automated chicken farm? A player calling himself Data has done exactly this – he's built a huge facility where caged chickens lay eggs, which hatch into chicks. These are then cooked with lava blocks when they're fully grown. Disturbing, but useful – and very tasty!

tinyurl.com/MCAnnual2018Build3

2 SHARK SUBMARINE

Movies like *Jaws* may portray great white sharks as villains but, let's face it, we all know they also look brilliant! They're fast, toothsome, and have a big, pointy dorsal fin that looks like a spoiler on a sports car. So what better way to live at sea than in a huge submarine shaped like a shark? This build is nicely appointed with a dining room, officer's quarters and sick bay, while you'll also find anti-aircraft guns and torpedo launchers – perfect for fending off shark hunters!

tinyurl.com/MCAnnual2018Build2

1 SELF-BUILDING CASTLE

Now this really is crazy! Pressing a button causes an entire castle to rise up out of the desert, as though it's being built before your very eyes. It's all powered by redstone – plus about 25,000 pistons – but the sheer brilliance of its design is beyond anything we've seen in Minecraft before. Jaw-dropping? If we didn't know better, we'd say it was magic!

tinyurl.com/MCAnnual2018Build1

HOW TO DO PIXEL ART

One fun thing to do in Minecraft is create pixel art. If you're not sure how, we'll show you all the tips and tricks!

FINDING A TEMPLATE

First decide what it is you want to recreate and figure out what blocks you'll need and how to arrange them. You can use Google's image search to find pixel art templates, or make your own by drawing a grid over a detailed image so you can turn it into a simpler one by shading the colour that makes up

A template looks like this

Put your design where it can be seen

Or you can build flat...

...so that your design looks good up high

most of each grid box.

When you've done that, you should know what colours you need as well as how many blocks.

STARTING TO BUILD

There are two ways to display your pixel art: flat on the ground or standing up. Building upwards makes the most sense because it's easier to see, but you might want to create a design that can be seen on the ground when players are high up (such the floor of your building).

If you want to incorporate pixel art into an existing world, find a decent spot to display it. High up is always good. Level the ground before you start, and make sure there's enough space.

Build your design carefully, row by row

Stick to your template and it will turn out great!

Before you begin putting down blocks, make sure you switch to Creative mode. Being able to fly makes building pixel art a lot easier (designs are usually very large!), and Creative gives you easy access to all of the blocks you'll need. Dyed or stained wool, concrete, clay and glass are best for coloured pixel art.

COPYING YOUR TEMPLATE

To copy your template, begin by counting out the blocks you need for the bottom row, and lay them out. Then add the next row on top. In some cases, it might be easier to fill in blocks of colour rather than row by row, but don't go too far. If you make even one mistake, it might throw off every other block you place!

Remember that it will be hard to see how pixel art looks up close, so copying your template very closely is the best way to get the image you want. It doesn't hurt to step back and make sure the design is working properly every few rows as you don't want to get to the end before you spot a mistake.

SHARING YOUR ART

If you want to take a picture of your creation when it's finished, just take a screenshot. Here's how:

Pocket Edition (iOS): Press the Home and Lock buttons together. The screenshot will be saved to your photoroll.

Pocket Edition (Android): The exact method depends on the device you're using, but usually you press the power and home buttons or power and volume buttons to save the screenshot to your photos folder.

Windows 10 Edition: Press the Windows Key and Print Screen together on your keyboard. The screenshot will then be saved to your screenshots folder (in the "pictures" folder).

PC Edition: Press F2. The screenshot will be then saved in the "screenshots" folder in your Minecraft directory (usually C:\Users\<your windows username>\ AppData\Roaming\.minecraft)

Console Edition: Use your console's built-in sharing/social function.

Stained blocks give you access to colours

Share screenshots for your friends to enjoy

BEAT EVERY MOB

There are loads of different enemies in Minecraft, so knowing how to beat them all is essential! Here are the best tactics for every hostile mob!

BLAZE

Use a bow and arrow to hit blazes while they're in the air, and carry a shield to block their fireballs. Eating an enchanted golden apple gives you five minutes of Fire Resistance, so is useful to have when fighting blazes.

Blaze

CAVE SPIDER

Cave spider

They're weaker than regular spiders, but can poison you with a bite. Arrows from a Flame-enchanted bow should let you keep your distance, and if you miss they'll hopefully incinerate some of the cobwebs that stop you getting to the monster spawner they emerge from.

CHICKEN JOCKEY

The easiest way to kill a chicken jockey is to jump off a ledge, wait until it follows and is in mid-air, then attack

Chicken jockey

the zombie on its back as it falls. Use a strong sword!

CREEPER

A simple tactic: run forward, hit the creeper with your sword so that it's knocked backwards, then back away fast. It will either take damage and not blow up, or you'll be far enough away from the explosion that it doesn't damage you.

Creeper

ENDERMAN

The best way to fight endermen is to wear a pumpkin to get close without them teleporting away. Don't bother using ranged weapons as they'll teleport away before you get a chance. They also ignore tame wolves, so they're invaluable in a fight against one!

Enderman

ENDERMITE

They're weak, so a couple of strikes with a sword should do. Don't waste potions or other consumable items on them as they don't drop anything good.

Endermite

Evoker

Ghast

Magma cube

EVOKER

Shoot them with a bow and use your shield to block vex attacks. Try not to get too close until they're weak – the fang attacks are very strong but won't work if you're far away!

GHAST

With the longest range of any normal mob (over 100 blocks!), Ghasts can be hard to fight. You can hit their fireballs back at them to cause damage, which results in a very powerful explosion. The secret is to hide behind blocks when you're not attacking as they can't see through walls!

GUARDIAN & ELDER GUARDIAN

Fighting guardians is very difficult due to their strength, spikes, laser attacks and the fact that they live underwater.

If you can wall them up and use a sponge to dry out the room that makes them easier to kill. Otherwise, get in close at one of their sides and hack away. Bring lots of enchanted armour and instant health potions!

MAGMA CUBE

Using a bow is the safest way to fight larger cubes, while smaller ones can be attacked with a sword. Never stay too close as magma cubes have double the attack rate of most mobs.

SHULKER

Wait for shulkers to open before attacking them – they're immune to arrows when they're closed, so don't waste any! Be careful if there are lots around – attack one shulker and others in the area will turn on you, so keep your back to the wall!

Shulker

Guardian

Silverfish

Skeleton

Slime

SILVERFISH

Hurting one silverfish will cause others in the area to emerge and attack, unless you kill the silverfish in one hit. For this reason, the best way to fight them is with an enchanted/diamond sword, to help avoid a swarm.

SKELETON

When fighting skeletons, use a shield to block their arrows then attack between shots with a sword or bow. If you don't have a shield, circle the skeleton while attacking and it should be unable to target you long enough to get an arrow on target!

SKELETON HORSEMAN

There's no great trick to killing horsemen – use projectiles and/or a bow and arrow to hit them – but if you attack and kill the rider you'll be able to take the horse for yourself.

SLIME

Large slimes split into smaller ones, so tackle them as they appear, otherwise you'll get overwhelmed. Always start by killing the smallest slime first. If you're fighting in a swamp, luring them into water is a great way to slow them down.

SPIDER

The best way to kill normal spiders is to wait until they chase you, then walk backwards while swinging your sword. When they jump at you they'll be hurt and knocked back, then be far enough away to try jumping again.

SPIDER JOCKEY

When fighting a spider jockey, attack the skeleton first. Spider jockeys are rare but very dangerous because both the spider and skeleton can attack you. The best way to deal with them is to focus on the skeleton as it's more dangerous.

Skeleton horseman

Spider

Spider jockey

Vindicator

Witch

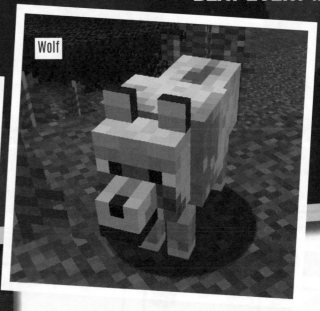

Wolf

VINDICATOR

Don't use a shield as their axes will disable it! Instead, use a splash Potion of Slowness to keep them in place, then hit them fast and often with your sword!

WITCH

Witches use potions to heal themselves and weaken you, so keep a bucket of milk to cure yourself. Use weapons that continue to inflict damage like fire, poison arrows/potions and lava to counteract their healing. Don't stop for a second, or they'll return to full strength!

WITHER SKELETON

The wither effect can be very dangerous and can even kill you, so don't let a wither skeleton near you. Use a bow and arrow to attack them, and throw splash Potions of Healing. Wither skeletons

have swords not bows, so if you keep your distance you should be safe.

WOLF

A pack of wolves will only attack if you provoke them first, so don't hurt them, but if you do the best protection is to get up high, usually in a tree. Don't try and fight them all at once!

ZOMBIE/ZOMBIE VILLAGER

Zombies are the easiest mobs to kill because they're slow and weak. Stick to using a basic sword – save stronger weapons for stronger mobs. If you're attacked by multiple zombies at once, a splash Potion of Healing can harm several in one go.

ZOMBIE PIGMAN

Because they carry swords, zombie pigmen can do a lot of damage. The best way to fight them is to climb on a two-block pillar then strike downwards. The pigmen will surround the pillar but be unable to climb it, so you can pick them off from above.

Wither skeleton

Zombie villager

Zombie pigman

31

PUZZLE

Blockdoku

Can you colour in the grid of blocks following these rules?

- Each small square must contain a coloured block
- Each of the brown rectangles must contain all SIX types of block
- No block type can appear on any line twice, horizontally or vertically...

32

PAGES PART 2

Super Sword Maze

Think you've got what it takes to plunder the pearl from our massive sword-shaped maze? Well, maybe you do... Just make sure you have plenty of supplies before you go in!

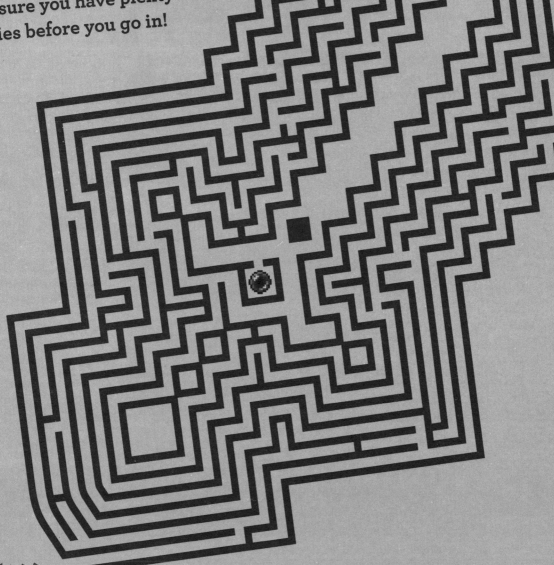

Start>>>

35 It's always worth adding extra lighting to a village to keep mobs away. You could even build a defensive wall around it if you want to keep the villagers safe!

36 Elytra can't be crafted, but you can repair them using leather on an anvil. Four leather will completely repair one set of elytra.

37 Don't repair any enchanted items on a crafting grid, otherwise you'll lose the enchantments. Use an anvil and raw materials instead.

38 Crafting minecart rails takes up a lot of resources and time, so when you stumble across an abandoned mine be sure to take as many of the unused rails as you can carry

A defensive wall

Be careful what you repair on an anvil

Don't anger a wolf!

back to the surface with you.

39 Don't bother killing baby animals when you come across them. They don't drop anything – not even experience – when they die, so there's no reason to waste your weapons on them. Wait until they're fully grown.

40 Wolf packs will actively hunt other animals, but they'll leave you alone unless you injure them. Hurt one and the whole pack will come for you though, so take care!

41 Rather than dyeing wool, find a sheep and dye it. This permanently changes the wool colour even after the wool regrows, so you can keep shearing your sheep for an unending supply of coloured wool.

Chickens will follow seed

Don't eliminate whole herds

Horses can heal by eating hay

42 Most animals will follow you if you hold a certain type of food. For chickens it's grain, for rabbits and pigs it's carrots, and so on. Use this behaviour to lead lots of animals at once so you can pen them in.

43 Always leave at least two animals in a herd alive so that you can breed more if you need to. Killing the whole herd is fine in the short term, but you'll regret it when you need the resources later!

44 If you walk too far from a tamed wolf it teleports next to you, so don't worry about losing it during a fight!

45 Horses, donkeys and mules can eat hay bales, healing up to 10 hearts. They're by far the most efficient way to restore your ride's health, so make sure you keep a few near your bases.

46 Feeding sugar to a horse has a variety of effects. It heals adult horses, makes smaller ones grow faster and helps wild ones tame more easily.

47 The moon's phases affect how mobs spawn, so pay attention. Full moons are the most dangerous – you'll see more slimes and stronger mobs, possibly with enchanted weapons, so prepare for a big fight!

Full moons raise the chance of equipped mobs spawning

48 On harder modes, zombies will look for and try to break down wooden doors. Use steel doors activated by a button to keep them out – they can't ever break through metal.

49 You can tell what profession a zombie villager had when it was alive, and you can use that to help you decide whether to kill it or try curing it. They might make a useful trading partner!

50 Once you've built a portal, there's a small chance of zombie pigmen spawning near it, so make sure it's built somewhere out of the way, if not fenced in completely. You don't want any nasty surprises!

Huge mushrooms give lots of food

have them to hand whether you need unique decoration or a source of dyes.

55 Large trees, like dark oak and jungle trees, can be grown by planting four saplings together then fertilising one with bone meal.

51 Despite their short appearance, baby zombies are faster and more powerful than regular zombies, and can fit through smaller gaps, so take them out first! Otherwise, you might miss them while you're trying to fend off the larger ones!

56 Cooked steak and pork chops are common food items that restore a lot of hunger points, so stock up on them, especially early in the game when you'll lose health quickly.

52 It's hard to grow mushrooms, but if you use bone meal to turn them into huge mushrooms you can harvest up to two mushrooms per block, and an average huge mushroom will yield around 14 small ones. You'll never go hungry again!

57 Save clownfish for taming ocelots. They have almost no other use and restore only a tiny amount of health if eaten, but will please ocelots as much as any other fish.

53 Cocoa pods only grow naturally on jungle trees, but as soon as you find one you can farm pods on any tree trunk. It doesn't have to be part of a tree!

58 If you want to clear things like grass, flowers and ferns, drop a water source block so that it spreads in all directions, then pick it back up. The ground will be washed clean.

54 When you find a flower forest, stock up on rare plants you can't get anywhere else. That way you'll always

59 Remember that armour only protects you from physical attacks. Fire, fall damage and

Cocoa pods are found in jungle biomes

Stock up on dyes in a flower forest

Dark oaks can only be grown from four saplings

Armour doesn't protect you from everything

A shield with a pattern on it

drowning aren't any less dangerous, though you can apply enchantments to armour pieces which will make them that way.

60
You can repair rare chainmail armour by using iron ingots on an anvil. Chainmail armour is slightly weaker than iron armour, but holds better enchantments.

61
Enchant books, rather than items, then combine the book with the target tool/armour on an anvil. It costs more, but you won't end up with enchantments you don't like on your valuable equipment.

62
Use shears on cobwebs to cut them quickly.

63
Learn to use the most appropriate tool to break blocks. Wooden blocks usually break fastest with an axe, stone with a pickaxe, and dirt with a spade.

64
Place your favourite type of arrow in your offhand inventory slot and your bow will prioritise those arrows. Otherwise, it takes them from the lowest numbered inventory slot.

65
You can combine a banner with a shield to transfer the pattern onto it. You can't remove the pattern or apply a new one though, so make sure you do it right!

66
Shields can't be enchanted directly, but you can apply Unbreaking to it by using an anvil and enchanted book.

67
When fighting the wither, create a distraction by building lots of golems. They can't do much to hurt the wither themselves, but it will attack anything it sees, and that will give you more time to attack it.

68
Destroy ender crystals with a bow and arrow while the ender dragon is healing itself with them and you'll deal a lot of damage.

CONTINUED ON P68

Rare chainmail armour

5 AMAZING POTIONS

There are LOADS of good potions

Smashing bottles o' enchanting releases experience orbs

Potions are cool ways you can boost your abilities, heal damage you've taken, or even cause damage to mobs. There are tonnes of different recipes, all with different effects and uses. Here, we look at some of the rarer potions that you might not know about!

For each potion, we give you the quickest recipe to create it – brew the ingredients into a water bottle in the order they're listed. Remember you may need blaze powder to power the reaction too!

BOTTLE O' ENCHANTING

Recipe: Can only be traded
This potion can be bought off cleric villagers if you trade with them enough to reach their highest trading levels. It costs between three and 11 emeralds. They can be thrown like splash potions and will drop experience orbs with 3-11 points. They're available in all editions, but at the time of writing trading isn't available in Pocket Edition, so they're only available in the creative inventory!
TIP: Don't just use these immediately – store them until you actually need them. Otherwise, if you die, you've wasted those emeralds!

POTION OF WATER BREATHING (EXTENDED)

Recipe: Nether wart, pufferfish, redstone
If you have to go on a long boat ride, it's worth keeping a Potion of Water Breathing with you because it means you can survive underwater. While the potion is active, your oxygen bar won't deplete. A standard one lasts for three minutes, but add redstone and it will last for eight.
TIP: The potion also slightly improves your ability to see underwater!

Water Breathing improves underwater vision too

Healing potions hurt the undead

POTION OF HEALING (LEVEL II)

Recipe: Nether wart, glistering melon, glowstone

The Level II Potion of Healing is the quickest way you can heal yourself (or most other mobs) because it instantly gives 8 points of health (4 hearts) when you drink it!

TIP: Add gunpowder to turn it into a splash potion – it will harm undead mobs like skeletons and zombies.

POTION OF LUCK

Recipe: Uncraftable!

The Potion of Luck can't be brewed, but is available in the PC and Console Editions inside the creative inventory. Drinking the potion increases the player's "luck" attribute by one point for five minutes. This means any treasure chests that are first opened while the potion effect is active are more likely to have rare or high-level loot in them.

TIP: To get the most out of the potion, drink it then fish for the entire duration of the potion's effect as fishing loot is also affected by luck.

POTION OF DECAY

Recipe: Uncraftable!

The Potion of Decay can't be brewed, but it's available in Pocket Edition if you use Creative mode. It inflicts the wither effect, which causes one point of damage every second (half of one heart) and lasts for 40 seconds. This means it can cause up to 40 points (20 hearts) of damage in a single use.

Unlike some health-sapping effects, a Potion of Decay is capable of killing you, so try and drink milk to cure it as quickly as possible!

TIP: It's best used as a splash or lingering potion – it's not like you want to drink this one yourself!

The Potion of Decay inflicts the wither effect

5 AMAZING RECIPES

Minecraft has loads of recipes, some of which you use all the time, and some of which you might never realise you can make. There are some super cool, rare and useful items in the game that are almost impossible to find but can be crafted easily – as long as you know what you need and how to get it!

To help you along, here are five amazing recipes you might want to try out.

An ender chest can't be looted

Crafting

ENDER CHEST
Use a crafting table to surround one eye of ender with eight obsidian blocks, and you create an ender chest. Every ender chest you build leads to the same storage area, so you can use them to store useful items you might want to access from lots of different places.

TIP: Every player has their own ender chest storage area, even when using the same chests, so you can use them to hide items from other players who might steal them!

ARMOUR STAND
Created from six sticks and a stone slab, armour stands can be used to display armour. They don't appear anywhere in the game, so you might not realise you can craft them, but you can!

They're mostly just for decoration, but you can use them to group suits of armour for easy access.

TIP: You can put mob heads and pumpkins on top of armour stands instead of helmets and caps, so you can use them to create little scarecrows or statues!

Turn an armour stand into a scarecrow!

FIRE CHARGE

Craft blaze powder, coal (or charcoal) and gunpowder together and you create three fire charges. You can't shoot them out of your hand, but you can put them in dispensers. When the dispenser is activated, it will shoot a fireball. They're also an ingredient in firework stars, allowing you to make fireworks!

TIP: You can use a fire charge to light a fire by "using" it on a block or mob in front of you, though it will use up the charge and could set you on fire too!

SLIME BLOCK

When you kill a slime, you can collect slimeballs, which can be crafted as part of leads, magma cream and sticky pistons. You can also craft together nine slimeballs to make a slime block. They slow down mobs and players, but if you jump

on one you don't take any damage and bounce back up instead!

TIP: Water flowing over slime blocks will push items faster than water flowing over normal blocks, so they're good for transporting things!

END CRYSTAL

To make an End crystal, you need one eye of ender, one ghast tear and seven glass blocks. They're only generated in the End where they heal the ender dragon, and can't be collected.

If you've killed the ender dragon, you can use End crystals to summon a new one by placing one on each side of the exit portal in the End. They can only be placed on obsidian or bedrock blocks.

TIP: End crystals explode when destroyed, so while they look cool, don't put them near anything valuable!

Slime blocks let you bounce!

Crystals can resurrect the dragon

AMAZING ENCHANT

Enchantments are one of the most fun things in Minecraft, because they give your items special abilities!

Enchantments can be applied to two groups of items or tools. Primary items can generate the enchantment spontaneously by being enchanted on an enchantment table. Secondary items can hold the enchantment, but only if combined with an enchanted book using an anvil.

Treasure enchantments are found only on enchanted books that appear in chests when fishing or when trading. At the time of writing, they're only in the PC and console editions, but will soon be added to the Pocket Edition!

UNBREAKING

Most items in Minecraft eventually fall apart through wear or damage, which makes Unbreaking invaluable.

Items enchanted with Unbreaking last several times longer than unenchanted ones. Level I Unbreaking makes items last roughly twice as long, while Level III Unbreaking makes them last four times as long.

Primary: Pickaxe, shovel, axe, sword, bow, fishing rod, helmet, chestplate, leggings, boots
Secondary: Hoe, shears, flint and steel, carrot on a stick, shield and elytra
TIP: Enchant diamond items – you get the most value from the enchantment that way!

Most enchantments can be applied like this

Unbreaking makes diamond items last almost forever!

FROST WALKER

This treasure enchantment can be applied only to boots, and allows the player to walk on water. At Level I, any water blocks within a three-block radius will be turned into ice. At Level II, the radius expands to four blocks. At both levels, it prevents the player taking damage if they walk over magma blocks.

Note that it can't be combined with the Depth Strider enchantment!
Primary: None
Secondary: Boots
TIP: Wear Frost Walker-enchanted boots when you visit the Nether!

MENTS

Frost Walker is a fun enchantment for boots

The Curse of Binding means you're stuck with what you're wearing!

CURSE OF BINDING

The Curse of Binding is a treasure enchantment that has only one level and can be applied to most wearable items.

Any item with the Curse of Binding is impossible to remove once the player wears it. The item can still break, and will fall off when the player dies, but once you put it on it stays on!

Primary: None
Secondary: Helmet, chestplate, leggings, boots, elytra, pumpkin, mob heads
TIP: Put cursed and weak items in a dispenser, and you can automatically equip them to people as a trap.

CURSE OF VANISHING

Another treasure enchantment, the Curse of Vanishing is a one-level enchantment that makes sure an item disappears as soon as the player dies, rather than getting dropped like a normal inventory item.

Primary: None
Secondary: Pickaxe, shovel, axe, fishing rod, helmet, chestplate, leggings, boots, sword, bow, hoe, shears, flint and steel, carrot on a stick, shield, elytra, pumpkin, mob heads
TIP: If you have a powerful weapon and don't want it to fall into enemy hands, the Curse of Vanishing will stop them – or you – getting hold of it after you die.

LUCK OF THE SEA

If you want to make yourself more likely to get the rare treasure enchantments, it's worth using the Luck of the Sea enchantment. This lowers the chance of catching junk and fish when you fish, and raises the chance of catching treasure, including enchanted books!

Primary: Fishing rod
Secondary: None
TIP: Combine with the Lure enchantment, which makes the rate of catches increase by up to 50% when fishing.

Items with Vanishing won't drop when you die

43

AMAZING ADD-ONS & MODS

One of the best things about Minecraft is how you can change it. Mods, skins, resource packs and add-ons allow you to alter the way the game looks and feels, adding amazing new visuals and features you might not have known about before.

But discovering which additions you want to use can be difficult. What's good and what isn't? To help you find out, we've collected together some of our favourites, and shown you exactly where to get them.

UNCRAFTING TABLE
(PC EDITION 1.11+)

This simple mod creates an "uncrafting" table that allows you to reclaim the resources used for any craftable item. As well as giving you a good way to reuse rare resources like diamonds, it gives you a cool way to get hold of raw resources. Unworn items return their full resources, while worn stuff might offer nuggets instead of ingots, or sticks instead of planks. You can even use it to recover enchantments by uncrafting an enchanted item with a book. It really changes the game in a fun way!
Download: www.minecraftmods.com/uncrafting-table

PLACEABLE ITEMS
(PC EDITION 1.10.2+)

Ever wished you could decorate Minecraft a little more and make rooms look more realistic? This mod turns most

Mods like Still Hungry let you add new things to the game

Uncrafting Table

of the items in the game into placeable items, meaning you can put 3D versions on top of blocks. Finally, you can set the table for meals, or leave books for people to read. You'll be surprised at just how much character it adds to the game!
Download: www.minecraftmods.com/placeable-items

Placeable Items

ocean, though you might need to drink a Potion of Night Vision and/or use the Respiration enchantment on your helmet or cap to make sure you can see properly once you're down there!
Download: mcpedl.com/ mine-submarine-addon

Mine-Submarine

MODERN TOOLS
(POCKET/WINDOWS 10 EDITION 1.0.4.1+)

This add-on adds six modern tools to Minecraft, replacing the shulker mob. You get a computer, which allows you to buy items off MineBay! There's a fridge that lets you store food. Plus more, like tables and chairs, and the forge, which turns coal into valuable items! The full details are visible on the download page, and we're sure you'll enjoy the extra additions this mod brings to your world!
Download: mcpedl.com/modern-tools-addon

MINE-SUBMARINE
(POCKET/WINDOWS 10 EDITION 1.0.4.1+)

Ever wished you could explore underwater a little more easily? Well, this submarine is just the item you need to do it! It's a controllable vehicle that stops you from drowning and allows you to visit the deepest part of the

JURASSIC CRAFT
(POCKET/WINDOWS 10 EDITION 1.0+)

Who doesn't love dinosaurs? This add-on for Pocket Edition includes 18 different dinosaurs, all with their own look and behaviour. Some you can tame and ride, others will attack you – there's even an official Jurassic Craft map to go with it. This is a huge mod with masses of additions, so you'll be able to spend hours playing with the dinos and seeing how you get on in a world full of them. It's like playing a whole new game of Minecraft!
Download: mcpedl.com/jurassic-craft

Modern Tools

Jurassic Craft

Modern HD

MineLoL

MODERN HD
(PC EDITION 1.10+)
This is one of the most popular resource packs ever, and was created by mikeyto1o to give Minecraft the appearance of a modern world. It's especially good for building houses and apartments that look like the kind you might find in real life. It's incredible what you can do with it, but it works best if you build new things with it rather than retexture your current builds.
Download: resourcepack.net/modern-hd-resource-pack

MINELOL (PC EDITION 1.10+)
Designed by casper033, MineLoL is a texture pack designed to make you smile. It does this by putting literal photos in the game, so if you want logs that look like real logs and fish that look like real fish, this is one way to go about it. The best things are the paintings, which have been turned into real-life wildlife photography. Check them out!
Download:resourcepack.net/minelol-resource-pack

PIXEL PERFECTION
(PC EDITION 1.10+)
This is a low-resolution (16x) texture pack designed to enhance the look of Minecraft on machines that don't have a lot of power. These redrawn blocks give Minecraft a whole new appearance without making huge demands on a low-resource PC. It's ideal if you want to improve the game's look but play on an older PC!
Download: resourcepack.net/pixel-perfection-resource-pack

PRECISELY PORTAL
(PC EDITION 1.10+)
Minecraft's cake is no lie, but if you want to pretend it is then this resource pack from Carlotta4th can help you turn your game into the futuristic testing facility you always wanted it to be.
Download: tinyurl.com/mw-portal

Pixel Perfection

Precisely Portal

Note: Console & Pocket Edition texture packs must be bought from the official store for that version. They're available on Android, iOS, Xbox 360, Xbox One, PS3, PS4, PS Vita and Wii U

Plastic

CITY (CONSOLE, POCKET & WINDOWS 10 EDITIONS)

Do you like making urban environments in Minecraft? Well now they can look the part thanks to the City texture pack, which doesn't just change your blocks – it also gives your mobs and villagers the appearance of office workers. There's nothing quite like seeing a creeper on their way to work!

PLASTIC (CONSOLE, POCKET & WINDOWS 10 EDITIONS)

Minecraft is a lot like LEGO, and if you want to get that LEGO-like appearance you can install this resource pack, which gives Minecraft's blocks a clean, smooth appearance that resembles your favourite building blocks. It makes things a bit easier to see too!

NATURAL (CONSOLE, POCKET & WINDOWS 10 EDITIONS)

Ever wondered what Minecraft might look like in real life? This texture pack makes everything look more like the thing it's supposed to resemble. We particularly like the leaves on vines, and the realistically coloured chickens!

CARTOON (CONSOLE, POCKET & WINDOWS 10 EDITIONS)

The cartoon texture pack doesn't look hugely different from the standard one, but it does give mobs funny-looking faces, and simpler versions of things like cobblestone, bricks and wood for a cartoonish appearance.

CANDY (CONSOLE, POCKET & WINDOWS 10 EDITIONS)

This texture pack turns your Minecraft game into a world of sweets and sugar! Check out the gingerbread golem, the chocolate Jack o' lantern, and dirt blocks that look like cake with icing on top.

Natural

City

Cartoon

10 TIPS FOR A BETTER BUILD

Want to make your creations in Minecraft look cooler than ever? Here are some tips to help you create better buildings!

1 LAY SLABS
If you have to create a large floor space, don't waste time digging up the ground and then laying blocks in it – just use slabs instead. Slabs double the area you can cover with your resources (i.e. three wood planks makes six slabs) and can easily be turned into steps that let the player walk up.

2 PLAN BEFORE YOU BUILD
To make sure your building looks good before you actually make it, why not plan your foundations first? You don't have to do this on paper – it can be as simple as building a wall plan on the ground before you start.

Lay slabs

Plan first

Stick to a theme

A sloped roof creates an attic inside!

3 PICK A THEME AND STICK TO IT
The best buildings look like they were made using the same kind of materials. If you want to build a castle, make sure your walls are built entirely out of stone-type blocks. If you're building a woodland hut, use only wood.

4 ADD A SLOPED ROOF
Sloped roofs look professional and give you the added bonus of creating an attic space inside! Stair blocks are useful for creating a sloped roof that's

Double doors look better than single ones

Experiment with windows

Make your buildings L-shaped

Build paths

Use slabs to create interesting floors

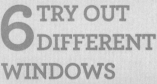
Automate your doors

also tall enough not to look stupid. Make sure it overhangs your walls slightly too!

5 PLACE DOUBLE DOORS

Double doors make it clear where the main entrance to your building is, and give an appearance of grandeur and scale that a single door can't. Try to pick the right kind of door – each type of wood creates a different looking one.

6 TRY OUT DIFFERENT WINDOWS

Windows are essential in any build, but that doesn't mean they have to be the same every time. Experiment with using different colours of glass, or blocks instead of panes. See what different effects you can achieve by combining different types!

7 DON'T MAKE ALL OF YOUR BUILDINGS INTO BOXES

In real life, houses are rarely just featureless cubes, and it's actually quite common for houses to be L-shaped. This allows you to split up the interior into different rooms and create interesting spaces on multiple levels. You could even have the top floor overhang the bottom one, like a Tudor house!

8 BUILD PATHS

It always looks good to run a path between things you've built. It will help you (and other people) remember where to go. Stone of some kind is usually your best choice. Try simple stone and/or stone slabs, though gravel is also a fun alternative because it makes a nice crunching sound when you walk over it.

9 DESIGN INTERESTING FLOORS

Whether you're using tiles, stone or carpet, making a design on your floor will improve an otherwise empty room. Tile symmetrical patterns for the best look, though you could also make pixel art if you're feeling creative. You'll be surprised at how much better it makes a room feel!

10 AUTOMATE DOORS

Put pressure plates in front of doors so they open and close automatically: when you approach a door it opens, and when you're through it closes. Just don't put them on the outside of your house, because zombies and other mobs can trigger them too!

EPIC MINECRAFT YOUTUBERS

Lots of people first heard about Minecraft by watching one of the thousands upon thousands of YouTube videos about the game. Here are some of our favourite YouTubers. Check them out if you haven't already!

SQAISHEY QUACK
www.youtube.com/user/sqaishey
What could be more fun than following the adventures of a yellow duck playing Minecraft?! Not many things. Sqaishey Duck is aimed at younger players, with a new video most days, including lots and lots of minigames!

Sqaishey Quack

LDSHADOWLADY
www.youtube.com/user/ldshadowlady
A channel that uses lots of mods to play Minecraft! Lizzie, the host, covers loads of other games too, and she loves Minecraft minigames!

LDShadowLady

BIONICMC
www.youtube.com/user/ItsBionicYT
If you've never seen the SkyWars and Factions mods for Minecraft before, BionicMC's YouTube channel is a great place to find out all about them! Follow the assorted battles here, and check out some of the mob grinder builds too!

BionicMC

THE ATLANTIC CRAFT
www.youtube.com/user/ TheAtlanticCraft
If you're looking for something a little more advanced, some of the videos you'll find at TheAtlanticCraft are just the ticket. They're hosted by TheCodyMaverick and JoeBuzz, and when you're done with their Minecraft

TheAtlanticCraft

DanTDM

work, check out their *Frozen* parody video, "Let It Glow"!

JEROMEASF
www.youtube.com/user/JeromeASF
You might want to get yourself a drink before you settle down to watch one of Jerome's videos as they tend to be on the long side. But then he's got so much stuff to get through, and he's a great way to get to know some epic mods for the game!

JeromeASF

POPULARMMOS
www.youtube.com/user/popularMMOs
You'll find some amazing stuff here, with brilliant Let's Play videos, mob and arena battles, and generally two new videos going up every day! You're bound to find something you like and, chances are, quite a lot!

PopularMMOs

THE DIAMOND MINECART
www.youtube.com/user/TheDiamondMinecart
For good reason, DanTDM is one of the most famous Minecrafters on the planet, and his YouTube channel has tons of Minecraft stuff on it (although he's also distracted by lots of other games!). You'll learn a lot watching The Diamond Minecart, and his videos are really good fun too!

STAMPY
www.youtube.com/user/stampylonghead
Probably the most well known Minecrafter on the planet, Stampy's YouTube channel is bursting with videos, with a new one added every day. His Let's Play videos are brilliant, and he's always looking for new series and ideas! No wonder millions of people subscribe!

Stampy

THE DEFINITIVE WORLD SEED

Seeds generate Minecraft's worlds

There are weird things to find...

...and cool sights to see!

WHAT ARE SEEDS?

Every one of Minecraft's infinite worlds has a world seed powering it. These are small strings of letters and numbers, and they're used to power the complicated algorithms that allow Minecraft to create its landscapes without storing tonnes of data. That's why you can download the game to your phone, tablet or PC without it taking ages!

WHAT ELSE DO THEY DO?

World seeds have another huge benefit: you can share them with other people so they can generate the same world. If you find something cool, sharing the seed lets other people see it too!

Each one is unique and special

HOW CAN I SHARE MY SEED?

World seeds can only be shared across versions that use the same algorithm, so Pocket, Console and PC editions can't use the same seeds. But if you're using the same edition as someone else, it's easy to generate the world they're in. Just enter the world seed in the advanced options when you create a new world.

HOW DO I FIND THE SEED I'M USING?

Every world you generate has a seed. To find the seed of the world you're currently in, type "/seed" into the console on the PC edition, or look on the World Options screen in Pocket Edition.

HOW MANY SEEDS ARE THERE?

On the PC, there are a total of 18,446,744,073,709,551,616 (18 quintillion!) seeds, each leading to its own unique world. Console, Pocket and Windows 10 editions have just 4 billion...!

GUIDE

Seed bigmountain

Seed 0

Seed -3500229128833691836

PC EDITION SEEDS

These seeds were all tested on version 1.11.2, but they should work on other versions too!

Seed: 0

Start near a massive desert with a large village that crosses into a grassy biome! Very rare. If you explore past the village, you can also find a desert temple and a savanna plateau with horses!

Seed: bigmountain

Starts you near a huge mountain range, overlooking a big flower forest! There are loads of biomes in this area, so it's a good place to start if you like seeing some really diverse things quickly.

Seed: -4589128118707775879

Woodland mansions can be tough to find, but this seed spawns you close to one! Walk in the direction you're facing when you spawn and you'll soon see it appear on the horizon.

Seed: -3500229128833691836

Want to check out some cold biomes? This seed starts you near a selection of cold taiga, ice plains and ice spikes biomes, and you'll be able to see polar bears and igloos, as well as fight strays without going very far!

Seed: 1461928132

This seed starts you next to what is probably the game's rarest biome – the mesa (bryce) desert – which has tall clay pillars, orange sand, and surface-level mineshafts!

Seed: -6980839137331707558

When you spawn, turn around and walk in the opposite direction, and you'll come to a place where a savanna meets a desert. On the left is a rare savanna village. On the right is a desert village with a ravine by it, and if you explore the ravine you'll find an incredibly rare fossil (at X:113 Z:-141)!

Seed -4589128118707775879

Seed 1461928132

Seed MCPE

Seed 106854229

Seed 65603

POCKET & WINDOWS 10 EDITION SEEDS

These seeds are tested on version 1.0.3, but should work on other versions too! Make sure the World Type setting is set to "infinite" – if it's set to "old" or "flat", you'll find yourself in a different world!

Seed: MCPE

This seed looks simple, but it usefully puts you next to a very flat grass plain, which is ideal for building large structures or small villages on without having to flatten the land first!

Seed: 65603

A fun glitch in this seed means the village spawns almost entirely on top of the water, giving you an easily defended and unique-looking home to start with.

Seed: 1407434958

Everyone loves a survival island, and this one gives you a good head start: there's a village right next to where you spawn. Will you try to make a life on the island, or try to escape? It's a fun twist on a classic Minecraft challenge.

Seed: 106854229

No list of seeds would be complete without one that started you next to the impossible-to-find mushroom island biome. Mushroom islands spawn no hostile mobs, so are a fantastic place to build up your inventory without any fear.

Seed: 1388582293

This huge settlement might look like a town, but it's actually three villages that have spawned right next to each other (which is why there are three wells – each well is the centre of a new village).

Seed: 805967637

The village near the spawn point of this seed might look normal, but if you empty out the well you'll see that it connects directly to the top of a stronghold. Break open the roof and off you go!

Seed 1388582293

Seed 1407434958

Seed -126880078651571709

Seed 5471950409906608474

CONSOLE EDITION SEEDS

All of the seeds listed below were tested and verified as working on the latest console versions we had access to: TU48 (Xbox 360), CU38 (Xbox One), PS3/PS4/PS Vita 1.41 and Wii U Patch 17. They should work on later versions too though!

Seed: -126880078651571709

Ever seen extreme temperatures side by side? This seed spawns you right next to a jungle biome, which is immediately connected to a cold taiga biome. Very strange!

Seed: -289973135

Survival island challenges are a great way to spend time on the Console Edition, and this is a pretty cool one! You start on a long island covered in trees, with plenty of resources and terrain to explore. It's a great place to get started!

Seed: -4718831715052553104

You'll spawn near a desert, which has a desert village containing a blacksmiths, so you can get your hands

on some awesome free loot. Then explore the nearby cave system to find a stronghold with a working End portal!

Seed: 5471950409906608474

Start near two of Minecraft's rarest features: an ocean monument and a mesa biome! Ideal for exploring things you might not have encountered before.

Seed: 5079366387731216932

If you're looking for igloos, look no further than this seed, which starts you not far from an ice spikes biome, which contains at least one igloo. There are also three villages and a desert temple within close distance, so you'll have a lot to find!

Seed: -671258039

If you hate looking around for diamonds, this spawn is a good place to start as the nearby village contains no fewer than NINE, meaning you can make a set of diamond tools or some pieces of diamond armour virtually as soon as you start the game!

Seed -289973135

Seed -671258039

PUZZLE

Crafting Crossword

Test your knowledge of crafting... Each question is a list of ingredients for a crafting recipe. Can you work out what they make?

Across
4. Seven sticks (6)
5. Two diamonds + one stick (7, 5)
10. Four obsidian + two diamonds + one book (11, 5)
11. Three wood planks + four cobblestone + one iron ingot + one redstone (6)
12. Four redstone + one glowstone (8, 4)
13. Three sugar cane (5)
17. Eight gold ingots + one apple (6, 5)
19. Four glowstone dust (9)
20. Three cobblestone + one blaze rod (7, 5)
21. Five glass + one Nether star + three obsidian (6)
22. Six matching wood planks (4)
24. (& 19 Down). Four leather (7, 5)
25. Eight obsidian + one eye of ender (6, 5)
26. Six wood planks + three books (9)
27. (14 & 6 Down). One iron ingot + one flint (5, 3, 5)

Down
1. Three bricks (6, 3)
2. Nine wheat (3, 4)
3. (& 18 Down). Three gold ingots + two sticks (4, 7)
6. See 26 Across
7. Two iron ingots (6)
8. One redstone + one stick (8, 4)
9. Five iron ingots (8)
14. See 26 Across
15. Four prismarine shards + five prismarine crystals (3, 7)
16. Three milk + two sugar + three wheat + one egg (4)
18. See 3 Down
20. See 24 Across
23. Five gunpowder + four sand (or red sand)

56

PAGES PART 3

Wordsearch

ALEX
BEACON
BIOME
CHICKEN
CRAFTING
DIAMOND
EMERALD
FURNACE
GIANT
GLOWSTONE
HORSE
IGLOO
JUKEBOX
LAVA
LLAMA
MINECART
MOOSHROOM
MOB
NETHERRACK
NOTCH
OCELOT
PIG
PISTON
POCKET EDITION
QUARTZ
REDSTONE
SHOVEL
SKELETON
STAIRS
STEVE
STORY MODE
STRONGHOLD
SWORD
VILLAGER
VIRTUAL
REALITY
WITHER
WOLF
ZOMBIE

K	H	R	Q	R	L	P	B	Q	A	M	O	W	L	O	X	U	W	N	J
P	A	P	O	C	K	E	T	E	D	I	T	I	O	N	Y	C	X	Z	G
Q	A	P	X	C	Q	M	H	V	O	U	G	M	P	P	T	K	K	T	L
L	N	Z	B	R	V	E	O	P	B	W	X	L	E	H	Y	L	L	Q	O
K	K	L	U	D	O	R	M	F	Y	I	W	D	O	B	F	D	Q	K	W
U	L	F	E	E	H	A	Y	U	K	T	N	H	C	O	R	A	A	H	S
W	N	M	M	T	U	L	Z	R	W	H	K	O	G	A	Q	U	V	D	T
L	F	O	M	H	M	D	Q	N	Q	E	U	U	B	B	G	T	O	Y	O
L	I	O	F	P	Q	O	C	A	K	R	E	R	O	S	S	L	F	K	N
B	N	S	A	J	E	W	I	C	M	T	F	Z	V	O	H	S	L	M	E
U	Z	H	L	E	H	O	R	E	B	X	L	Q	B	F	S	O	T	S	I
O	P	R	D	L	B	E	A	C	O	N	Z	S	S	P	Y	H	R	P	N
K	T	O	F	A	A	R	C	G	A	X	R	B	T	J	E	E	M	S	H
O	X	O	U	V	L	M	Y	G	R	R	W	C	F	W	G	S	B	V	E
I	X	M	T	A	Y	E	A	B	G	W	D	O	D	A	P	K	M	I	A
Z	C	G	J	S	B	J	X	B	P	P	I	G	L	S	T	E	F	L	J
K	H	F	W	U	M	W	O	E	T	Z	A	L	E	F	H	L	R	Z	U
V	I	R	T	U	A	L	R	E	A	L	I	T	Y	N	Q	E	A	N	K
W	C	A	O	Q	B	D	S	F	J	V	U	Q	A	T	C	T	V	O	E
I	K	B	H	D	E	X	T	A	E	B	Y	R	T	W	O	O	M	O	B
E	E	B	D	N	K	I	A	F	Z	X	N	L	U	K	B	N	D	E	O
F	N	I	R	L	G	K	I	Z	N	P	F	A	I	F	M	Z	Y	D	X
M	Z	T	K	S	T	O	R	Y	M	O	D	E	C	K	A	M	H	G	Z
G	O	J	Q	O	O	K	S	N	F	Y	B	S	B	T	W	L	J	L	T
C	M	I	E	C	R	A	F	T	I	N	G	T	T	N	O	Q	K	W	H
C	B	N	I	W	U	E	W	Y	Q	B	J	R	X	O	C	U	B	A	L
U	N	E	T	H	E	R	R	A	C	K	A	O	M	T	O	A	W	K	U
E	E	N	E	E	N	N	W	O	F	J	K	N	I	C	C	R	Z	I	R
N	O	V	B	D	I	A	M	O	N	D	S	G	N	H	S	T	E	V	E
B	M	B	E	R	N	W	P	C	C	H	X	H	E	G	L	Z	V	T	D
Z	L	S	W	O	R	D	L	E	S	H	F	O	C	H	I	V	M	Q	S
S	P	W	T	B	V	C	Z	L	X	F	A	L	A	Y	K	W	S	N	T
Y	F	S	D	E	R	U	T	O	V	P	W	D	R	O	E	T	U	X	O
B	I	L	V	G	I	A	N	T	X	E	J	M	T	G	X	W	I	Q	N
P	T	X	A	X	G	B	P	T	U	V	C	X	N	P	T	X	I	J	E

HOW TO MAKE YOUR OWN MINECRA

The PC edition of Minecraft allows you to make your own skins, and the good news is that your computer already has the tools you need! Here's how you can come up with your own character design and put it in the game!

1. DOWNLOAD A SKIN TEMPLATE

You can easily find these on the official Minecraft wiki: **minecraft.gamepedia. com/Skin**. The skin file will look something like the image below, as if you've taken the character model and laid it out flat.

you edit the legs and arms individually instead of putting the same skin on both.

2. EDIT YOUR SKIN FILE

You can use any image editor to do this, but we're going to show you how to do it in Windows Paint because most people have that!

First, open the file. Zoom in, because it makes it easier to see – 64 pixels is a very tiny amount! You may also want to turn on gridlines (click "view", then tick "gridlines") so you can see the pixels more easily.

The skin is divided into sections, which correspond with bits of the character model in-game. We've numbered them, and here's what those numbers mean. Anything not numbered is ignored!

We're using the simple version, which is 64 x 32 pixels, but there are also bigger versions (64 x 64 pixels) that let

FT SKIN

1. Face
2. Top of head
3. Right of head
4. Left of head
5. Bottom of head
6. Back of head
7. Front of leg
8. Top of leg
9. Right of leg
10. Left of leg
11. Bottom of leg
12. Back of leg
13. Front of body
14. Top of body
15. Right of body
16. Left of body
17. Bottom of the body
18. Back of body
19. Front of arm
20. Top of arm
21. Right of arm
22. Left of arm
23. Bottom of arm

Paint anything you like on the skin, though try to make sure the edges match up. It can be tricky! Rather than make a skin from scratch, we've just changed the colours on the original. You can be more daring, though. Maybe recreate a favourite character from a movie, comic or TV show?

When you've finished editing, save your skin using an original filename, making sure it's in the PNG file format.

3. UPLOADING YOUR SKIN

To use your skin in Minecraft, you have to log into your account on Minecraft.net and upload it. Click "log in", then when you've entered your password, click your email address and choose "profile".

You'll see the following screen.

YOUR PROFILE

CHANGING THE WAY YOU LOOK IN-GAME ON PC/MAC

Change your skin

Give your character a unique texture! Create your own skin or find ready-made skins on the internet! Check out this help article for more information.

First choose the shape of your Minecraft character by picking one of two models:

Classic (Steve)

Then upload your skin:

Drop your skin file here, or   select a file   to upload.

Want to go back to the default look?

Reset skin

Select the shape of your character – either Classic (Steve) or Alex – depending on the skin you started with as a base. Now select the skin file by either dragging it into the dotted box or clicking the "select a file" button and finding it on your PC.

If you get no error messages, click "upload" and you're done!

If you get an error message, try to correct it. The file needs:

■ A resolution of 64 x 32 or 64 x 64 pixels
■ To be about 2k in size
■ To be saved in the PNG format, with 16-bit depth.

4. LAUNCH MINECRAFT

If the upload worked, you'll see a "success!" message in green. Now run the game and you'll see your skin in action!

If you ever want to remove it, just log into your profile again and click "Reset Skin".

AMAZING MINECRAFT RECORDS

While some of these may have been beaten by the time you read this, here are some formidable challenges for those of you who want to be the world's best at Minecraft! These records have all been verified by the *Guinness Book of Records*.

> LONGEST MINECRAFT GAMING MARATHON

Martin Fornleitner, who spent – get this! – 24 hours and 10 minutes playing the game back in 2011. Yikes!

> LONGEST TUNNEL IN MINECRAFT

In 2013, Lachlan Etherton of Australia built an incredible tunnel that ran for 10,502 blocks and took 10 minutes just to walk through! Since then, in March 2017, someone even beat that.

ItzEpicGeorge built a 100,000-block tunnel that at game walking speed takes over six hours to get through!

> LONGEST MINECRAFT JOURNEY

You can keep walking for ever and ever if you really want to in Minecraft, and Kurt J Mac must have felt he was doing just that when he started exploring the Far Lands (which were removed from the game in version 1.8, but Kurt keeps an old version running). He had walked over 2000 km in the game as of 2015, and you can follow his ongoing efforts at **farlandsorbust.com**

Stone Titans: largest pyramid built in Minecraft

Diversity 2: most downloaded Minecraft project

> MOST SURVIVAL GAME WINS

Minecraft player gravey4rd had notched up 2,534 wins as of September 2013. That record has since stood for years!

> MOST DOWNLOADED MINECRAFT PROJECT

As of early 2016, this was Diversity 2, created by qmagnet, a special map that challenges you to complete a monument. You can find it here:

www.planetminecraft.com/project/ diversity-2-multi-genre-map

> LARGEST PYRAMID BUILT IN MINECRAFT

Containing 2,629,176 blocks, Stone Titans' pyramid took over a year to build, and is a full reconstruction of the Great Pyramid of Giza. It was declared a world record on 2 November 2013.

> FASTEST TIME TO BUILD A HOUSE

Here's a record you can easily try: the fastest time to build a house using Pocket Edition! The record was set by Tristen Geren of the USA in October 2015. It took him three minutes and two seconds.

> TALLEST STAIRCASE BUILT IN ONE MINUTE

Another Pocket Edition record, Lestat Wade of the USA built a 29-step staircase in 60 seconds in October 2016. The condition of the record is the player must be able to walk up all the steps without having to jump!

Far Lands: longest Minecraft journey

SUMMONING SECRET MOBS

Minecraft has more mobs than you know about, and some of them can only appear if you cheat! If you're using a version of Minecraft that has an in-game console, you may be able to make a secret mob appear. Here's what you need to do!

Sorry Console Edition players! Right now, the only way to summon these mobs is to use the in-game console on the PC, Pocket and Windows 10 editions.

ACCESSING THE CONSOLE ON PC & WINDOWS 10

To access the in-game console on the PC or Windows 10 editions, press the forward slash key. On a normal keyboard, it's in the bottom right, between ">" and right shift, on the same key as the question mark. Enter the summon command given and the mob will appear!

ACCESSING THE CONSOLE ON POCKET EDITION

On tablets and phones, getting to the console is easy: press the speech bubble icon at the top of the screen (next to the menu icon) and then type the forward slash followed by the command given. It will even autocomplete for you!

GIANT ZOMBIE

The giant zombie – aka the giant – is an oversized zombie six times as tall as a normal one. They stand 12 blocks high

Enter the console commands like so

/summon giant_

A giant is taller than a church!

but otherwise look identical to other zombies. Here's how you summon one:
PC: /summon giant

Although giants have been in the game for some time, they never spawn on their own. They have no AI, so when summoned they'll stand still, facing south, and won't move unless pushed or hit. They can be killed, though! Giants have 100 hit points, and drop 5 experience points, just like a normal zombie.

The zombie horse is green

ZOMBIE HORSE

Although Minecraft allows players to encounter the skeleton horse naturally, there's another variant of the horse – the zombie horse – which doesn't spawn in the game without you summoning it, and that's the zombie horse.

To summon a zombie horse, type the following command into the console:
PC: /summon zombie_horse ~ ~ ~ {Tame:1}
Pocket & Windows 10: /summon zombiehorse

Unfriendly zombie horses can't be tamed, so if you want to ride one you'll have to summon it tame already. They always have 15 health (the lowest possible value for a horse), can't ever breed, and won't eat food! When killed, they drop rotten flesh instead of leather, and 3 experience like a normal horse.

KILLER BUNNY

Added at the same time as rabbits, the killer bunny is a hostile variant of rabbits, which is in the game as a reference to a scene from the movie *Monty Python and the Holy Grail*. It has all-white fur and horizontal red eyes. There are friendly white rabbits in the game, so don't get confused if you think you've seen one!

To summon a killer bunny, type the following command:
PC: /summon Rabbit ~ ~ ~ {RabbitType:99}

When spawned, they'll attack any player in a 16-block radius, moving quickly and jumping to cause damage, much like a spider. They're immune to the Thorns enchantment, and won't despawn if the game is set to Peaceful!

Killer bunnies don't mess around!

DAY VS

When you're in Survival mode, you can do lots of things at any time of the day in Minecraft. But there are some things that happen only during the day or at night...

DURING THE DAY

- A day in Minecraft lasts for 10 minutes, followed by 90 seconds for sunset.
- It's much easier to see! All blocks directly in view of the sky will grow a light level every 10 seconds as the sun rises.
- Spiders become instantly hostile towards you at night, but during the day? They'll leave you alone unless you attack them!
- Zombies and skeletons will burn during the day, unless they can find shelter.
- Most passive mobs will spawn only during the day, when the game's light level is at least 9 (15 is the maximum, 0 is the minimum).
- Blocks such as wheat, carrots, melons and potatoes will grow once the light level gets to 9 during the day.
- Grass and mycelium will spread to adjacent dirt blocks once the light is at 9 or higher.

Daytime lasts 10 minutes

NIGHT

AT NIGHT

◖ A night in Minecraft lasts seven minutes, followed by 90 seconds for sunrise.

◖ Beware the hostile mobs that spawn in the dark. The likes of zombies, skeletons and spiders come out once the sun has set.

◖ Villages aren't safe. Zombies have a habit of spawning and killing the villagers!

◖ Stay close to light. Monsters don't spawn in the light, so make sure you have some Jack o' lanterns or torches.

◖ Try and find shelter to keep safe at night, and make sure the shelter is lit!

◖ Slimes are more likely if there's a full moon.

◖ If you're struggling to get through the night, perhaps switch the game to Peaceful mode. That way, no more mobs will spawn, and you'll regenerate health.

◖ That, or make yourself a bed, and sleep through the night. Crops won't grow if you do this, though.

Mobs spawn when the sky goes fully dark

Full moons raise the chance of equipped mobs spawning

HEROBRINE: MINECRAFT'S BIGGEST MYSTERY!

Who or what is Herobrine? And have you seen him?!? Tens of millions of people play Minecraft every year, and they travel across the game's vast, expansive lands, exploring, fighting, building and occasionally seeing something just a little unusual!

It was in the earlier days of Minecraft that a player first reported seeing something we've now come to know as Herobrine. The player was chopping wood and saw something moving in the fog. Because he was playing on a slow PC, the graphics settings were fairly basic, but still he chased the mystery figure and saw someone who looked like Steve, but wasn't Steve! Instead, it was a Steve skin, but with no name above his head and nothing where his eyes were supposed to be.

Excitedly, the player tried to post about what he'd seen, but he reckons the post kept getting deleted. Then he apparently got a message from a player going by the name of Herobrine. The message simply said: "Stop"!

THE MYSTERY DEEPENS

Further claims were made that Herobrine was the brother of the creator of Minecraft, Notch. Notch reportedly replied, saying that his brother had died. However, Notch has strongly denied this, saying on Twitter that "I don't have a dead brother" and that "he never was in the game".

That didn't stop other reports of Herobrine sightings from appearing though, but, as you might expect, there were a lot of hoaxes! People were using programs such as Photoshop to put Herobrine

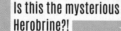

Is this the mysterious Herobrine?!

Another sighting?

WHAT DOES HEROBRINE DO?
According to stories, Herobrine will:
- Create odd and random things, such as long 2x2 tunnels
- Cut all the leaves off trees
- Run, but he can't fly
- Take control of passive mobs, and sometimes revive undead mobs
- Not enter the Nether or the End

into screenshots and pass them off as real. That said, a live stream by a player called Copeland appeared to show Herobrine in a house. Another user, Patimuss, reckoned they met Herobrine in a live stream too in the middle of a lava field!

SO IS HE REAL?
No he's not. The two streams – from Copeland and Patimuss – were eventually revealed to be fakes. Furthermore, the Minecraft team – both old and new – have been adamant that Herobrine was never in the game.

People have even gone right the way through the programming code that makes up the Minecraft game, and found no reference at all to him. Not that the programmers aren't up for pulling

people's legs: often, when they do an update to the game and release accompanying notes, they write "Herobrine removed" in there! Mojang has also been known to slip a picture of Herobrine into, for instance, the background of a banner advertising the official Minecon convention!

However, just because people have been told that Herobrine doesn't exist, it doesn't mean everyone believes it! People still claim to see Herobrine fairly regularly, and some users have put together their own Herobrine-themed builds to get in on the fun.

Unofficial mods to the game have also played around with him. While things like that continue, Herobrine will always be the unofficial ghost of Minecraft!

Signs Herobrine has been busy...?

First claimed sighting

101 MINECRAFT TRICKS PART 3

69 If villagers get injured by mob attacks, you can heal them by using a splash/lingering Potion of Healing or by trading an item with them. It's faster than waiting for a new villager to spawn and/or grow to adulthood!

Mob spawners are rare

Take a shortcut through the Nether

70 Monster spawners are rare and can be really tricky to find, but destroying one gets you more immediate experience than anything else in the game. Well, other than killing a boss creature!

You can walk on lilypads

71 It can be useful to carry a bed with you when exploring the Overworld so that you can wall yourself up and skip nights. Just be careful to stay alive. If the last bed you slept in doesn't exist, you get sent back to the world's spawn point.

72 Never try to carry too much when you're exploring underground. Use chests to create small temporary storage areas. Otherwise, if you die before you make it back to base, you'll lose everything!

73 You can build shortcuts through the Nether to travel long distances and save time!. Every step you take in the Nether is equivalent to eight steps in the Overworld, so journey times are massively shortened, though it's obviously a lot riskier!

74 You can walk on lilypads while they're floating, so they're a great way to get out of the water for a bit or make simple bridges.

Remember to pull up the carpet in igloos

An exposed diamond vein

Watch out for silverfish

75
Boats are faster than walking, so if you're travelling or exploring a new area, sticking to water will allow you to cover more ground than clambering over uneven terrain.

76
Remember to pull up the carpet in igloos to see if they've generated a basement. Only 50% of igloos have basements, though!

77
Diamond ore veins can generate diagonally, so break all of the blocks around any piece of ore you find to make sure you don't miss this valuable block.

78
If you're in extreme hills, a stronghold or an igloo basement, watch out for monster egg blocks. They look normal, but break a little slower than you expect and release silverfish when they're finally destroyed.

79
If you encounter a dead end while exploring, you might want to block it off with a bar of cobblestone so that you don't accidentally go down there again. Place a torch on the front so that if you ever encounter it from the other side, you know where you blocked it off from.

80
It's quicker to discover diamonds in caves than it is to mine for them. They usually appear near underground lava lakes, so follow the edges of those and you should then find some diamonds quite easily.

Soul sand can trap players and mobs

81
If you need to blow up some TNT, don't just set it on fire with a flint and steel then run. Use redstone dust to create a "fuse" and activate it from a safe distance with a redstone charge (i.e. a redstone torch).

82
Soul sand makes mobs (and players) stick to it, so you can trap them by surrounding soul sand with slabs that let them in easily, but stop them stepping out.

83
Using a nametag on a mob prevents it from despawning, though it's still possible for it to die. If the mob is hostile, it will also disappear if you set the difficulty to Peaceful, so don't be surprised if you do that.

You get one gateway per dragon kill

see what's around them. The location is marked by a green blob.

88 You don't have to put coal in furnaces. Almost anything wooden can burn, including saplings, so it's a useful way of getting rid of junk and hanging onto valuable coal.

84 Soul sand will suffocate silverfish and endermites, causing them to die. You can use this knowledge to trap silverfish in strongholds.

89 If you want to collect lots of snow, build a snow golem in a small pit or dark room (making sure it doesn't get too hot!) and it will generate a layer of snow as it wanders around, which you can easily harvest.

85 You can submerge yourself in water to largely escape the effects of TNT or a creeper explosion – they'll barely touch you!

90 Incinerators are useful for getting rid of blocks, but fire and lava can cause severe damage to you and your base. A cactus block, however, will destroy items that touch it but can't set anything on fire, so it's a lot safer!

86 End gateways only generate when you kill an ender dragon. You can use them to teleport around the End by throwing ender pearls into them. Every ender dragon you kill generates a new End gateway, and when you travel through one it generates an exit gateway so you can get back.

91 You can cast fishing rods onto pressure plates to set them off from a distance.

87 Make a map of your base area and place it on the wall in an item frame so that any visitors to your world can easily

Make a map of your base!

Careful if you use lava as an incinerator

Snow golems leave snow where they walk

Netherbrick fences are more efficient

You can wash off dye in cauldrons

Leather Tunic

92
If you're making fences, remember that six Nether bricks will create six Nether brick fences, whereas six sticks will create only two wooden fences.

93
Don't use glass blocks as windows. Six glass blocks make 16 glass panes, so you cover more space using them!

94
Netherbrick fences don't join up to wooden fences, so you can use a Netherbrick fencepost to create a gate that lets you through but keeps animals penned in.

95
Cauldrons can be filled with water and used to wash the dye off leather clothing, or fill three glass bottles.

96
You can expand villages by building shelters with doors. Each new door increases the chance of a new villager spawning.

97
You can force most trees to always grow tall by planting the saplings in holes three blocks deep.

98
Beacons can be built overlapping to save resources, as long as the beacon blocks at the top are at least a block apart.

99
Destroy the pressure plate in desert temples as soon as you find them, otherwise a mob might spawn and set off the TNT!

100
You can build an End portal in Creative. Just make sure the portal blocks are all facing the right way (with the lines pointing inwards), otherwise it won't activate properly!

101
Polar bear cubs spawn naturally, but there's no way to breed polar bears, so don't try!

Glass panes are more efficient windows than blocks

You can't breed polar bears

71

SPLOSH!

CALLUM! BRING BACK MY TABLE CLOTH, THIS INSTANT!

My glasses! I can't see a thing without them!

The Creeper is onto me. Need to put on this mob head, to decrease the Creeper's detection range!

THUD!

SPLASH!

Look at the state of this! And where are your glasses?

Yikes! The Creeper's gonna explode!

Right! Back to your spawn point young man. You're grounded for the rest of the weekend.

Bah! Ocelot of fuss about nothing!

END!

75

MINECRAFT JOKES

WHAT DID THE CAT SAY WHEN IT WAS GIVEN THREE DINNERS AT ONCE?
Ocelot of food!

WHAT DID STEVE SAY WHEN ALEX ASKED HIM IF HE WANTED TO LEAVE THE OVERWORLD?
I Nether do!

ALEX BROUGHT A LOT OF ROCKS HOME.
She picked them herself!

DID YOU HEAR ABOUT THE MINECRAFT MOVIE?
It's a blockbuster!

RECKON YOU'VE GOT ANY BETTER RIB-TICKLERS THAN THESE?!

STEVE WAS TELLING STORIES OF ALL THE HOSTILE MOBS HE'D BEATEN. They did drag-on!

ALEX BUILT A HOUSE, BUT IT WAS QUITE SMALL. Steve said "there's not mooshroom here"!

WHAT'S A CREEPER'S FAVOURITE TIME OF YEAR? Christmassssssssssssssssss!

WHAT'S IT LIKE TO HAVE A FIREBALL FIRED AT YOU IN MINECRAFT? Ghast-ly!

WHAT WOULD STEVE AND ALEX DO WITHOUT TREES? They wood not know!

MINECRAFT'S EASTER

Dinnerbone

A pig named Dinnerbone

Minecraft contains loads of secrets, easter eggs and in-jokes. Here are some of the best we could find! They definitely all work on the PC edition and on many of the other versions too.

HALLOWEEN MASKS

On 31 October, any mob that can wear armour – zombies, skeletons, pigmen and wither skeletons – can spawn wearing a pumpkin or Jack o' lantern. You can collect the blocks by killing the mob with a sword carrying the Looting enchantment, otherwise they disappear when it dies.

Also, the only splash text on the title screen on Halloween is "OOoooOOOoooo! Spooky!"

UPSIDE DOWN MOBS

If you use a nametag to give a mob the name "Dinnerbone" or

"Grumm" (with a capital letter) it turns upside down. Dinnerbone and Grumm are two of Minecraft's developers!

MULTICOLOURED SHEEP

If you use a nametag on a sheep to rename it "jeb_" (no capitals, with an underscore) then its wool will cycle through every available colour.

Jeb is the lead designer for both Minecraft and Minecraft Pocket Edition, responsible for adding many things to the game: pistons, wolves, villages, strongholds – you name it!

TOAST THE RABBIT

Another variant mob can be created by using a nametag to call a rabbit "Toast" (with a capital letter).

Toast looks quite similar to other black and white rabbits, but has more black fur on its face. It was added to the game by Minecraft developer Ryan Holtz to commemorate the missing rabbit of Minecraft user xyZenTV.

Mobs wearing pumpkins

EGGS

Toast

Toast, the unique rabbit skin

This cake isn't a lie, at least!

KILLER BUNNY

The killer bunny mob is hostile to players, wolves and dogs. It can only be added to the world using the summon console command.

MINCERAFT

There's a 0.01% chance that the title screen will read "Minceraft" instead of Minecraft. It was added to the game by the original developer, Notch, but nobody noticed for years!

PORTAL REFERENCE

The achievement you get for crafting a cake is called "The Lie". This is a reference to the game Portal, which spawned the slogan "The Cake is a Lie".

ENCHANTING SYMBOLS

The enchantment symbols are actually from the "Standard Galactic Alphabet" invented by Tom Hall for the 1990s computer game, Commander Keen.

BROKEN RECORD

If you've ever tried to play Disc 11 in a jukebox, you'll remember it as the broken record that plays a weird and distorted tune. There's actually a secret behind its music: if you run the sound through a spectrogram – a program that turns soundwaves into visible waves – you can see a picture of a Minecraft character's face. Some speculate that this is actually the face of the mysterious ghost Minecrafter, Herobrine!

It's also possible to see the number "12418", which is a reference to Minecraft's soundtrack composer, C418. The number "12" represents the letter "C" in the computer language of hexadecimal.

Does the broken record contain the face of Herobrine?!

These enchanting symbols are actually letters!

PUZZLE

Picture Grid

Use the grid to help you finish the second picture, then colour them in however you like!

PAGES PART 4

Nonograms

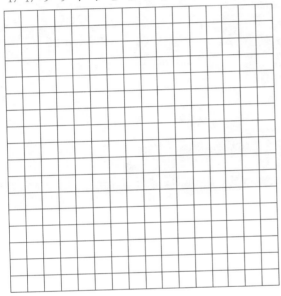

Nonograms are puzzles that use blocks. There are a few different names for them, so you may know them as Hanjie, Picross, or even Griddlers! They're all very similar, though.

The grids need to be coloured in using the numbers. These numbers tell you how the squares need to be coloured in on that column. If you do it right it will reveal a picture of a Minecraft mob...

The colour of the numbers is a suggestion of the colour you should use to colour in the blocks. So, if the number sequence of a row is '2 2 2 2', you would need to colour in two brown squares together, two green, two green and two more brown.

Craftymaths

Why not use some squared paper and a calculator to help you work out these Minecraft maths problems?

1. If you wanted to build a house that's 15 blocks long on every outside wall, and every wall is five blocks high, how many blocks will you need to build the walls?

A:_____

2. If you wanted the bottom two blocks of the walls to be quartz, how many of those blocks would you need?

A:_____

3. How many blocks would you then need to make a floor inside the empty house?

A:_____

4. If you then used one-block thick walls to divide the house into four equally sized rooms, how many blocks would each room have on the floor?

A:_____

BRILLIANT MINECRAFT LEGO SETS!

Looking for some more Minecraft fun once you've switched off your computer, tablet, phone or console? Then try some of these amazing LEGO sets!

ICE SPIKES
Brrr! Just looking at this set gives us the shivers. It features lots of snow, an enchantment table and a nasty spider out to get you!

Nether Railway

FORTRESS
A really fun set, with fires, torches, cannons and golden armour all helping you to defend an impressive fortress. We love the lookout towers!

Ice Spikes

Fortress

NETHER RAILWAY
Dare you brave a trip to the Nether? To be on the safe side, this LEGO set gives Steve diamond armour and a diamond pickaxe. The real fun is with the minecart, though!

Iron Golem

Mushroom Island

IRON GOLEM

Iron golems are a lot of fun in the Minecraft game itself, and they're a lot of fun in LEGO too. This set comes with a baby pig, a furnace and a zombie, which should keep your iron golem busy!

Dungeon

MUSHROOM ISLAND

Head out to sea with this set, as you get to build your own mushroom island. Watch out, though: there's an exploding creeper that wants to spoil all your fun!

VILLAGE

There's a lot going on in this LEGO Minecraft village, with friendly and, er, less friendly mobs! The set comes with a library and marketplace, amongst other things.

DUNGEON

Beware! There's a mob spawner lurking in this LEGO set, which also comes with a trio of minifigures and some gold ore to mine.

Village

THE BIG MINECRAFT

Reckon you know Minecraft? See how many of these questions you can get right! Find out how you did on page 90!

1 An easy one! Who are the two main characters you choose from at the start of a game of Minecraft?
A. Steve & Alex
B. Steve & Andrea
C. Shane & Alex
D. Shane & Andrea

2 Which mob makes a hissing sound before it blows up?
A. Zombie
B. Ender dragon
C. Witch
D. Creeper

3 Who is the man credited with inventing Minecraft?
A. Steve
B. Shane
C. Alex
D. Notch

4 Which of these is a popular Minecraft magazine?
A. Minecraft User
B. Minecraft World
C. Minecraft Insider
D. Minecraft Today

5 Which of these mobs in Minecraft is tameable?
A. Zombie
B. Shulker
C. Guardian
D. Mule

QUIZ

6 Which biome features a flat landscape, steep hills and mycelium instead of grass?
A. Beach
B. Desert
C. Mushroom island
D. Taiga

7 Who do you trade with in Minecraft?
A. Villagers
B. Cows
C. Sheep
D. Spiders

9 What do you need to smelt to make charcoal in the game?
A. Grass
B. Fruit
C. Wood
D. Carrots

8 Which of these is a type of golem in Minecraft?
A. Snow
B. Ice
C. Fire
D. Rain

10 What do you need for electricity in Minecraft?
A. Redstone
B. Fire
C. Lightning
D. Food

11 If you kill a creeper using a skeleton's arrow, what special item will it drop?

A. Nether star
B. Chest
C. Feather
D. Music disc

14 What should you put on your head in the game if you want to look at an enderman without it attacking you?

A. A potato
B. A pumpkin
C. Grass
D. A melon

12 One of the most popular Minecraft YouTubers is DanTDM. But what does TDM stand for?

A. The Dastardly Minecrafter
B. The Dazzling Minecraft
C. The Diamond Minecraft
D. The Digging Man

13 What's the name of the company that published Minecraft?

A. Activision
B. Mojang
C. Data East
D. Psion Software

15 If lightning strikes within 3-4 blocks of a creeper, what does it become?

A. A charged creeper
B. An electrical creeper
C. An angry creeper
D. A savage creeper

16 Which mob do you need to defeat to get a Nether star?

A. Ender dragon
B. The wither
C. Zombie pigman
D. A creeper

17 What burns forever if you ignite it in Minecraft?

A. Charcoal
B. Grass
C. Netherack
D. Trees

18 What's the name of the episode-based spin-off game that first launched in 2015?

A. Adventure Mode
B. Spectator Mode
C. Education Edition
D. Story Mode

19 In real time, how many minutes does a day last for in Minecraft before sunset?

A. 6 minutes
B. 8 minutes
C. 10 minutes
D. 12 minutes

20 What's the name of the annual Minecraft convention?

A. Minecon
B. Minecraft Convention
C. Mine
D. Minecraft Live

SSSHHHH! EXPERT MIN SECRETS

Wanna play Minecraft like an expert? Here are six secrets you can use to improve your game in no time!

Get experience!

◼ Farmland can turn back into dirt

You might know that farmland turns back into dirt if it dries out, but it can also be trampled by mobs and players. Avoid jumping on your crops, and you'll keep the farmland blocks ready for planting, saving both time and effort!

◼ Learn the best ways to get experience

Experience in Minecraft is hard to get, because you only get a small amount for everything you do. You can get the most from destroying a monster spawner, but a better option is to dig a large, deep pit beneath the spawner. Mobs will appear then instantly fall, and as long as they're injured but don't die you can easily kill them and get XP.

◼ Build several furnaces

There's no way to speed up the time it takes to smelt a block or cook an item, but that doesn't mean you can't hurry things up. Furnaces are cheap to make (they only need cobblestone and a fuel source), so don't be afraid to build several. Every extra furnace you build halves the total time it takes to smelt the number of blocks you need, so we recommend building at least four for any reasonably sized project.

Mobs can trample farmland

Don't mine when underwater!

ECRAFT

Fishing in the rain means you get bites quicker

Multiple furnaces speed up smelting

Don't mine in water

You can find useful blocks underwater, most notably clay, but mining it isn't advisable since when your top half is submerged, you mine five times slower than when you're on dry land. Even worse, mining blocks underwater can create an undercurrent that stops you swimming fast enough to escape – leave too little time to return for air and you'll drown!

Any expert player knows that there are two things you can do to fix this. You can use enchantments, like Aqua Affinity, to make your time underwater a little easier on you. Or you can place certain items, like doors and fenceposts, which create air pockets underwater that you can stand (and breathe!) in.

Fish when it rains

You can skip rainstorms by sleeping, but experts know that the best time to fish is in the rain. It improves the catch rate of any rod, meaning you're more likely to get your hands on treasure and food. Fishing already takes a long time, so you should only fish during good weather if you're

desperate for food (or fancy relaxing).

You can combine this effect with the Luck of the Sea enchantment for even better results while fishing!

Explore smarter

Getting lost in a cavern is an amateur move for sure. The best way to keep track of where you're going without any extra work is to put torches on only one side of a cavern – left or right is fine, as long as you stick to that. Now, when you want to get back to the surface, just make sure the torches are on the other side of you and you'll be led all the way back without getting stuck.

Put torches on one side of a cave to find your way out

ANSWERS

Dot-To-Dot

Quiz

1. A
2. D
3. D
4. B
5. D
6. C
7. A
8. A
9. C
10. A
11. D
12. C
13. B
14. B
15. A
16. B
17. C
18. D
19. C
20. A

HOW DID YOU GET ON?

- **0-4 CORRECT:** A good try, but there's a lot more for you to find out about Minecraft yet!
- **5-10 CORRECT:** Not bad, but room for improvement!
- **11-15 CORRECT:** You know your Minecraft, don't you? Well done!
- **16-19 CORRECT:** Brilliant! You're a Minecraft expert in the making!
- **20 CORRECT:** Wow! We're in awe of you! Epic work!

Craftygrams

1. Polar bear
2. Rabbit
3. Snow golem
4. Silverfish
5. Magma cube
6. Endermite
7. Chicken jockey
8. Wither skeleton
9. Ender dragon
10. Elder guardian

Spot The Difference

Blockdoku

Sword Maze

Nonograms

Craftymaths

1. 280
There would be two walls of 15x5 blocks (75 blocks each, so 150 in total), but the other two walls would be 13x5 (65 blocks each, 130 in total)

2. 112
Each layer would be 56 blocks (15+15+13+13), so two rows would be 112. Alternatively, working out 2/5 (or 40%) of 280 will give you the same answer.

2. 169
The inside of the building would be 13x13 blocks once you take away the walls.

3. 36
Dividing the building with a cross in the middle would leave four rooms measuring 6x6 blocks.

13 Blocks

6 Blocks

15 Blocks

Wordsearch

Crossword

MINECRAFT FACTS

To finish, here are a few Minecraft facts you can use to ~~bore~~ fascinate your friends and family!

MARKUS 'NOTCH' PERSSON
The man who came up with Minecraft!

17 MAY 2009
The day the first ever test version of Minecraft was released for people to play.

18 NOVEMBER 2011
The day the full version of Minecraft was officially released!

$2.5 BILLION
The amount Microsoft paid to buy the company behind Minecraft, Mojang, back in 2014!

DANIEL 'C418' ROSENFELD
The man behind the music of Minecraft.

MINECON
The name of the annual, official Minecraft convention.

OVER 8 MILLION
The number of subscribers Stampy has on his YouTube channel.

2019
The year the official Minecraft movie is set to be released!

OVER 120 MILLION
The number of copies of Minecraft sold worldwide, and growing every day!

365 The number of days we expect to be playing Minecraft in 2018!